D0846614

WORLD'S BEST

(AND WORST)

SPORTS JOKES

EMMA CARLSON BERNE

Lerner Publications ◆ Minneapolis

Q Why did the chicken cross the road during the soccer game?

A He couldn't stay in the game—he'd been kicked out for fowl play.

Lerner Publications Company
A division of Lerner Publishing Group, Inc.
241 First Avenue North
Minneapolis, MN 55401 USA

For reading levels and more information, look up this title at www.lernerbooks.com.

Main body text set in Billy Infant Regular.
Typeface provided by SparkyType.

Library of Congress Cataloging-in-Publication Data

Names: Berne, Emma Carlson, author.
Title: World's best (and worst) sports jokes / Emma Carlson Berne.
Description: Minneapolis : Lerner Publications, [2018] | Series: Laugh your socks off!
Identifiers: LCCN 2017011783 (print) | LCCN 2017027382 (ebook) | ISBN 9781512483598 (eb pdf) |
    ISBN 9781512483536 (lb : alk. paper)
Subjects: LCSH: Sports—Juvenile humor.
Classification: LCC PN6231.S65 (print) | LCC PN6231.S65 B47 2018 (ebook) | DDC 818/.6020803579—dc23

LC record available at https://lccn.loc.gov/2017011783

Manufactured in the United States of America
2-45732-33171-5/2/2018

The football player called a time-out.

What's going on? asked his coach. I thought you were enjoying this game at the wildlife park. There are elephants, giraffes, and hippos too!

The football player shook his head. It's no use, Coach, he said sadly. There are just too many cheetahs.

Q **Where do football players like to buy things?**

A The tackle shop.

>>>>>>>>>>>>>>>>>>>>>>>>>>>>>>>

Q **Why was the football coach mad?**

A He wanted his quarterback.

Knock, knock. Who's there?
Tess.
Tess who?
Tess me the football. I want to play!

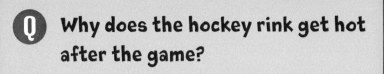

Q Why does the hockey rink get hot after the game?

A Because all the fans have left.

Q What is a hockey player's favorite chess move?

A Checkmate.

Q What game do hockey players like to play during recess?

A Puck-Puck-Goose.

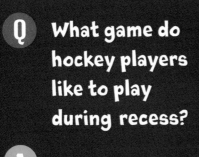

KNEE-SLAPPER

Q What job does a skeleton do at a hockey game?

A He drives the Zam-bony.

Q What position on the soccer field is most popular at Halloween?

A Ghoul-ie.

Q What did the angry soccer ball say to the striker?

A Stop kicking me around!

Q What do you call a goal made by a triceratops?

A A dino-score.

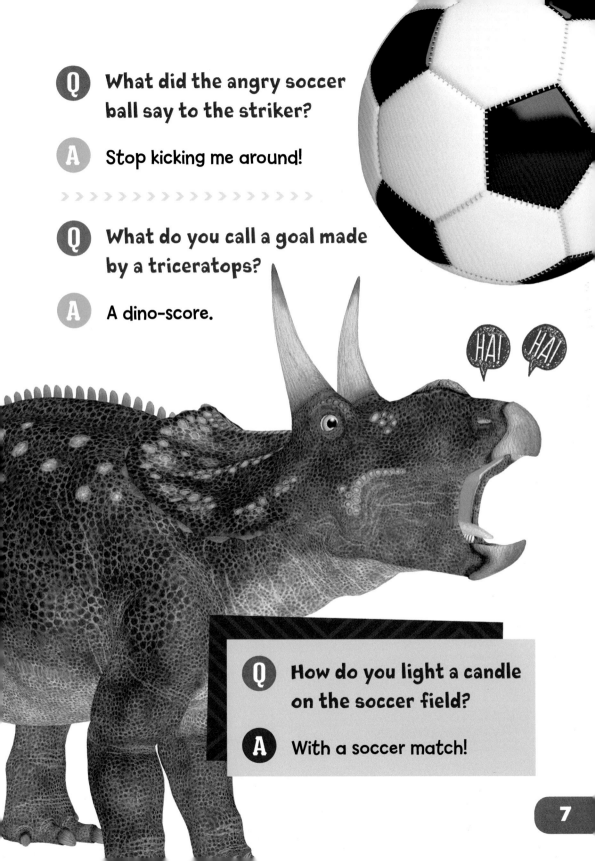

Q How do you light a candle on the soccer field?

A With a soccer match!

Q What do frogs like to do at baseball games?

A Catch fly balls.

Q What runs all the way around the field but never moves?

A The fence.

KNEE-SLAPPER

I really need to hire some help! said the pastry chef, Chris.

What kind of help? asked the dishwasher, Dave.

I'm thinking of hiring a baseball pitcher, Chris said.

Why? Dave asked. You're a chef!

Well, a pitcher will really know how to handle the batter.

Two police officers run onto a baseball field.

What are you doing here? asks the manager.

We had to check things out, the officers answer.

WE HEARD SOMEONE WAS STEALING A BASE!

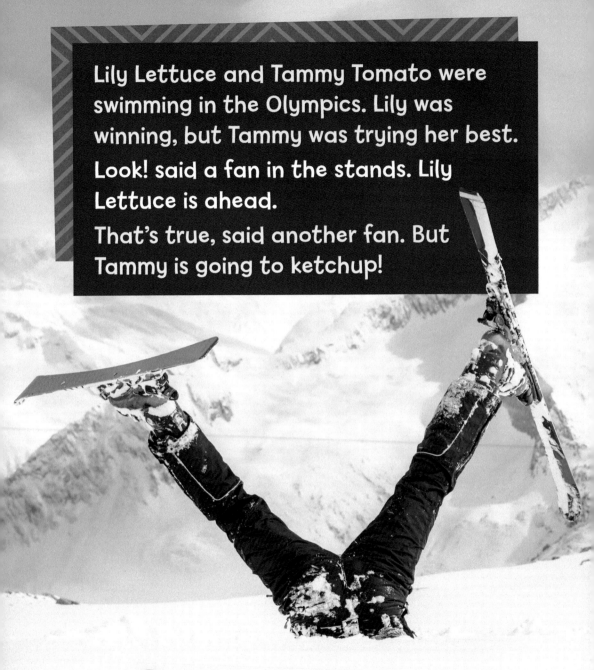

Lily Lettuce and Tammy Tomato were swimming in the Olympics. Lily was winning, but Tammy was trying her best.

Look! said a fan in the stands. Lily Lettuce is ahead.

That's true, said another fan. But Tammy is going to ketchup!

Q Why was the Olympic ski race a disaster?

A It was all downhill from start to finish.

Q Why did the music-loving Olympian cry?

A Because she broke her own record.

GROANER AWARD

The Hot Dog Olympics were almost over. The announcer turned on the loudspeaker.

Attention, please! he shouted. Will all the wieners please report to the podium?

Sara's track coach walked up to her after the meet.

You know, Sara, he said, I remember when you were afraid of hurdles. What's helped you?

Sara shrugged. Coach, I just got over it.

Q How did the barber win the cross-country race?

A He took a shortcut.

>>>>>>>>>>>>>>>>>>>>>>>>>

Q What is harder to catch the faster you run?

A Your breath!

Q What did the **STAR WARS**-obsessed sprinter say to his teammates before the race?

A **MAY THE COURSE BE WITH YOU!**

Q You know why track-and-field competitors are so chatty?

A They're always discus-ing.

Q What is a heavyweight's favorite kind of dog?

A A boxer!

Knock, knock. **Who's there?**
Raoul.
Raoul who?
Raoul with the punches—this is a boxing match!

Q What is a boxer's favorite part of a joke?

A The punch line.

A boxer sat down in a barber's chair.
What kind of haircut today, sir? asked the barber.
An uppercut, of course! answered the boxer.

GROANER AWARD

Q How do you make a cranberry punch?

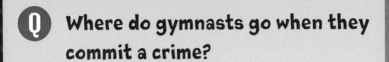

Q Where do gymnasts go when they commit a crime?

A They wind up behind bars.

Q What did the gymnast say when she stepped into the **STAR TREK** transporter?

A **BEAM ME UP, SCOTTY!**

Q How are gymnasts like bananas?

A They can both do splits!

Q Why don't vegetarians go to gymnastic events?

A They don't like meets.

HA! HA!

Two dinosaurs were watching a car race when one car spun into another. Oh no! one dinosaur said. What went wrong?

These things happen, the other dinosaur answered. It was a tyrannosaurus-wrecks.

Q Why did the wheel take a nap after the car race?

A It was really tired.

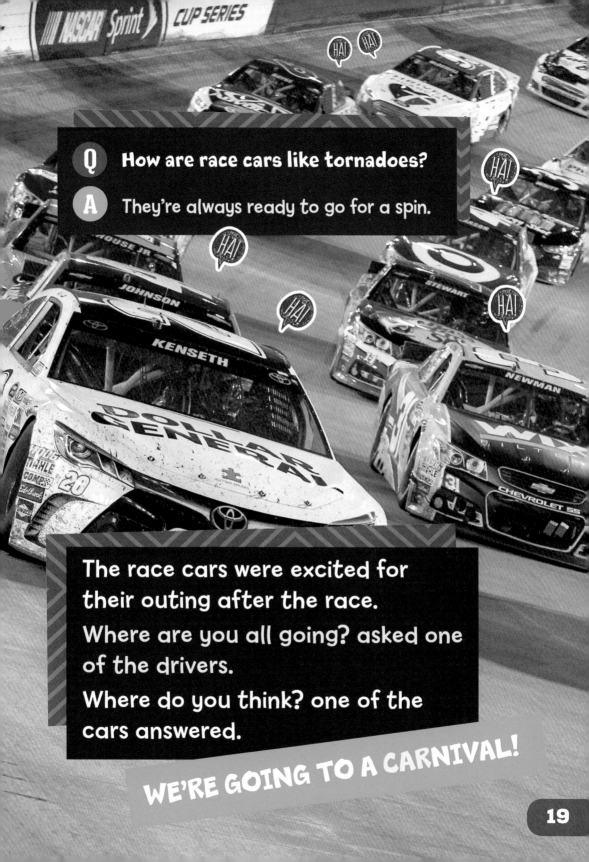

Q How are race cars like tornadoes?

A They're always ready to go for a spin.

The race cars were excited for their outing after the race.

Where are you all going? asked one of the drivers.

Where do you think? one of the cars answered.

WE'RE GOING TO A CARNIVAL!

Q Why did the wave rider take his laptop into the ocean?

A He wanted to surf the Internet.

Q Why did the surfing chicken cross the beach?

A To get to the other tide!

Delaney and Jen were paddling out to surf. Delaney noticed that Jen was carrying some strange items.

Jen, Delaney said, why do you have tape, glue, a hammer, and nails with you?

Jen sighed. Oh, Delaney—in case the waves start breaking, of course!

Q What do surfers love to do at baseball games?

A The wave.

Grandma Kathy was walking down the sidewalk when a little girl on a bicycle crashed into her.

Lisa! Grandma Kathy said. Don't you know how to ride your bicycle?

I'm so sorry, Lisa replied. I do know how to ride my bicycle. I just don't know how to stop!

Knock, knock. Who's there?

Willy.

Willy who?

Willy make it through the Tour de France?

Q What do you get when you cross a bicycle and a flower?

A Bicycle petals.

GROANER AWARD

Q What did the little bicycle call his dad?

A Pop-cycle!

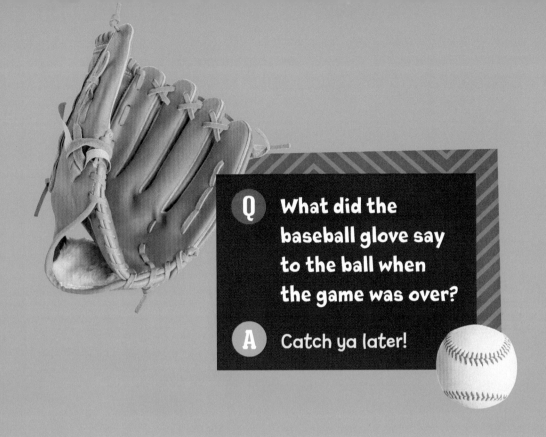

Q What did the baseball glove say to the ball when the game was over?

A Catch ya later!